MATIA ISLAND

ORCAS ISLAND

LUMMI ISLAND

SINCLAIR ISLAND

BLAKELY
ISLAND

GUEMES
ISLAND

CYPRESS ISLAND

DECATUR ISLAND

ANACORTES

LOPEZ ISLAND

SAN JUAN ISLANDS

SAN JUAN ISLANDS

Photography by Ed Cooper

Text by Ruth Kirk

GRAPHIC ARTS CENTER PUBLISHING COMPANY
PORTLAND, OREGON

*End paper map copyright 1972 The Pargeter Company and
reprinted with permission. Copies of map with additional
nomenclature and information available from The Pargeter
Company, P.O. Box 844, Kent, WA 98301.*

Acknowledgement
I would particularly like to thank Gary Craig, whose help in
getting me to many of the smaller islands assisted greatly
in contributing to the success of this book. I also thank Louis Kirk
for the photographs on pages 26, 31, 39, and 112.
Ed Cooper

Page 2: The intricacies of San Juan Islands' waterways perfectly match the scale of pleasure craft. Everywhere, you see boats anchored or moored or tied at finger slips, such as these at the West Sound Marina of Orcas Island.

"There's no danger of turning into an LA here," says an island developer. "There's no major employment, just beauty. The place promotes itself." Schooner anchored in Richardson Bay at Lopez island.

Small islands—the biggest here is less than 180 square miles—retain their ocean identity. Whether driving, afoot, or riding a bicycle, you are almost constantly in sight of salt water, as here on Shaw Island.

Above: Churches built in pioneer days are loved, kept up, and—often—still used. This one, at Center on Lopez Island, dates from 1881. *Overleaf:* For residents, the islands offer livelihood and home. For yachtsmen, even windless days when sails remain furled bring release from the cubbyholes and constraints of everyday life.

Above: Once glacier ice nearly a mile thick overrode the islands. Among its signatures are rounded peaks, many of them now well forested. *Right:* Madrone trees *(Arbutus)* present an exotic beauty apparent even in the bark. *Overleaf:* The roofline of the 1904 Congregational Church in Lopez Village serves as a landmark whether approached from the water or on land.

Change within the islands is enormous, but its pace is slower than on the mainland and less strident. You realize—through contrast—the tempo elsewhere. *Above:* The west side of San Juan faces Vancouver Island, British Columbia. *Left:* From Matia you look south to Lummi and Orcas islands.

Scheduled boat service to the islands began in 1873 with the arrival of a mail boat every other week, while en route between Whatcom (Bellingham) and Port Townsend. Today four Washington State ferries make daily calls. The hotel at Orcas Landing, third stop outbound from Anacortes, offers meals but no longer is a hostelry.

SAN JUAN ISLANDS

We're at 1,000 feet in a Cessna flying to Rosario on Orcas Island. With us is ninety-year-old Herb Evison visiting from Pennsylvania. Years ago he knew Robert Moran, the Seattle shipbuilder and ex-mayor whose white mansion is now Rosario Resort. Herb and his wife even were guests of the Morans sixty years ago. We're taking him back now for dinner. He never before has crossed Puget Sound by small plane, but he recognizes landmarks, remembers names. Suddenly he sings out "Whidbey Island" as we fly over the Clinton Ferry just leaving its dock. Then it's "Oak Harbor" as we're above a crescent of buildings turned to pink boxes by the low angle of the sun, which is about to splash down into the Strait of Juan de Fuca between Washington State and British Columbia.

Herb sits forward, watching eagerly. He spots the 500-foot cliffs of Deception Pass and the cantilevered and arched bridge joining Whidbey Island to Fidalgo Island. Driving to the airport he'd told us about when Deception Pass State Park was dedicated; about when the act setting up the state park system passed the Senate in the closing fifteen minutes of the 1921 legislative session; about Robert Moran donating thousands of acres on Orcas Island for Moran State Park, scant months after the passage.

"That would be Anacortes," Herb says now, pointing beyond Deception Pass. Mount Baker looms virginal in the distance, a reddening triangle above the round storage tanks of the oil refinery. Two freighters approach the coast nearby. Between them and the sleeping volcano, the Skagit River delta spreads like a mammoth green apron: sediments eroded from the Cascade Range, now flat and farmed and with a brown plume of silt-laden water spewing from the river mouth. Such sediment continually pushed the delta seaward another ten to twenty feet per year until controlled by present diking and channeling. Poets speak of the "eternal hills" but they are misguided. Time equals change. The substance of today's delta formed yesterday's peaks.

At dinner Herb tells of the last time he was in the Moran mansion. We sit at a window overlooking the darkened bay, a sprinkling of small boats tied to mooring buoys. Candles pool yellow light onto white tablecloths; a pianist plays melodies from the 1920s. Herb laughs. "We'd camped for a week at Cascade Lake, then hiked to the top of Mount Constitution to watch the sun come up over Mount Baker. After that the Orcas Island game warden and I went fishing while our wives picked Astrachan apples in an abandoned orchard and put up jelly.

"Next we came here to the Moran 'palace.' Fifty-four rooms! At breakfast Mrs. Moran laid a beautiful juicy slice of ham onto a plate for our Airedale but the dog took that meat over there, onto the middle of a — probably priceless—rug. I jumped up. Mrs. Moran said not to bother. Let him enjoy it. That was in 1921."

Change. Yet, ironically, timelessness is the soothing essence of these islands, a siren call luring admirers whether resident or transient. The question is how well the loveliness can keep pace with the lovers. "Stoplight? Ha," boasts the headline of an article in the current summer tourist issue of Friday's Harbor's *Journal*. "There isn't a single stoplight in the whole of San Juan County ... and we hope it stays that way." There is,

however, an elevator. It's located in the new shopping mall and a second elevator is planned for the courthouse addition.

Definition of the San Juan Islands isn't easy to pin down. Partly the problem depends on whether you're thinking of high tide or low. Figures quoted vary from source to source but the *Journal* issue with news of stoplights and elevators reports that at low tide there are 768 islands, rocks, and reefs; at high tide only 457. Of these, 175 have names, 50 have people.

Where the line encircling the San Juans lies depends on who you're talking with. Some favor including islands like Guemes, Cypress, and Fidalgo. I don't. Particularly not Fidalgo. You can drive to Anacortes and that's counter to my first criterion of San Juan-ness, which is that there can be no bridge. Arrival by water or by air is the only acceptable way. My line ringing the San Juans runs up Rosario Strait to the Strait of Georgia and then along the border with Canada. This cuts off British Columbia's Gulf Islands, which topographically are inseparable from the San Juans but politically must be set apart. From the Gulf Islands my line lies down Haro Strait to the Strait of Juan de Fuca. Within this area, twenty-five miles across, lie four main islands — Orcas, San Juan, Lopez, and Shaw — plus half a dozen satellite islands such as Blakely and Waldron. There's also a score of outliers like Matia, Patos, and Stuart; and uncountable dots with names like Puffin Island, Cactus Island, Skull Island, Posey, Dinner, Swirl, Iceberg, and a host of others, equally evocative.

Drawing the official lines onto the San Juan map very nearly set off a war in 1859. Spain, Russia, England, and the young United States for decades had each sought control of the western edge of the continent. In 1819 Spain finally pulled south as far as California. Five years later Russia gave up North American claims except for Alaska. That left England and the United States. Hoping that the Columbia River would become the ultimate boundary between the two, British Hudson's Bay Company traders built Fort Vancouver on the river's north bank. But in 1846 the Oregon Treaty instead set the 49th parallel as the international boundary.

In the San Juans the line officially ran down "the middle of the channel which separates the continent from Vancouver's island; and thence southerly to the middle of the said channel, and of Fuca's straits to the Pacific Ocean." All might have been well except that nobody specified *which* channel marked the line, Rosario or Haro. Each nation of course chose to assume the one giving it the islands. And to add substance to assumption, each nation encouraged its citizens to settle in the islands.

On San Juan, Hudson's Bay Company started a salmon salting operation and soon added a sheep farm. Trouble began when the Washington Territorial Legislature, newly independent from the jursidiction of the old Oregon Territory, decided to levy customs duty on whatever Hudson's Bay Company brought to the island. HBC refused to pay. The county sheriff therefore seized thirty-four sheep and started to auction them at facetiously low prices to partly cover unpaid duty. HBC men arrived armed with knives to rescue their stock. Sheriff and settlers resisted with pistols. Even so, nothing much happened. Then an American adrift after the boom-and-bust Fraser River gold flurry picked San Juan Island as the ideal place to grow potatoes. Unfortunately, a HBC pig strayed into his potato patch and the new settler, Lyman Cutlar, promptly shot the vagrant beast.

Captain George E. Pickett, later of Civil War fame, landed with sixty-seven men on July 27, 1859 in response to islanders' fear of retaliation. Their arrival quickly brought 2,000 British troops including Royal Marines and artillerymen to glower from ships' rails at the entrenched American troops, by then reinforced to 460 men. Luckily the only shot actually fired was the one that killed the pig, though for thirteen years England and America each maintained a post with 100 men on San Juan. Only ten miles apart and with nothing serious in contention, rivalry centered on outdoing one another in hosting a series of sumptuous dinners.

At length Kaiser Wilhelm I of Germany agreed to arbitrate the boundary issue and the center of Haro Strait became the international line. The venerable Union Jack fluttered down the pole at Garrison Bay and the San Juan Islands became American. Today you can visit the reconstructed British blockhouse and barracks near the northern end of San Juan Island and the earthen redoubt of Pickett's men at the southern end.

Fisherman's Bay, Lopez Island – May 18

Our small sloop *Taku* pulls gently on the anchor line as the tide changes and a night wind blows across the low sand spit separating this bay from the main waterway between San Juan and Lopez Islands. There's no worry, however, about the anchor holding. This bottom is sand; the hook is well set.

We're making our first sail of the season, only the two of us aboard. My husband Louis is so content at the boat's tiller, I suspect salt water flows with the blood in his veins. My own *forte* is the galley more than the cockpit. I know sheets from halyards but seldom tie proper knots and start each cruise silently translating port-left, starboard-right.

We sailed here this morning: twenty-five nautical miles in four hours, Port Angeles to Cattle Point, site of the 1860s American military camp. The point's name comes from a Victoria cattle ship that wrecked here in pioneer days, releasing its startled cargo. Most of the beasts swam for shore and successfully waded up the beach. No descendants remain. The land now is administered along with the English blockhouse and camp site as a national historic park. No farming goes on where Hudson's Bay Company pigs once foraged. The grassy-brown slope is dotted with occasional white, however, as though sheep still grazed. But there's no shearing these white dots. They're stone; granite boulders carried here from Canada 14,000 years ago as glacier ice capped most of British Columbia and spilled over onto adjacent lowlands.

I commented to Louis that American Camp looks exposed, as though it were Pickett's first landfall, as ours. He responded that it is a good defensive position. How oddly obscure islands command their moments on center stage. The San Juan islands in the 1860s, The Falklands in the 1980s. What gives American Camp present-day fame, however, are skylarks that pour out song in flight: feathered English imports well adjusted to American life, the only nesting skylarks in Washington.

Now we are anchored off Lopez Island. At teatime we rowed ashore and walked the road a mile to Lopez Village and Holly B's Bakery. Sit on her porch with a chocolate croissant and, although neither tempo nor view suggest the Champs Elysées, remembered taste and aroma transport you. Lopez Village isn't where people live; it's a cluster of businesses and a post office, a center for greetings and gossip while collecting mail and stocking up on groceries. A concrete block building set in a mowed field houses the Lopez Historical Museum, its weathervane an iron miniature of a reef-net rig, the unique regional fishing method. This afternoon the museum was closed, its secrets of the past secure. Each major island has such a museum and we've never managed to see inside. Local love is easier to come by than budget, so how can it be otherwise?

A red, wooden watertower across from the Lopez museum is now a thrift shop. A single watertower next to the supermarket is a dwelling. The old red schoolhouse has become the community library (also closed). A sign proclaims the gleaming white Congregational Church with its four blockish towers as built in 1904. It's closed too but tended and in apparent weekly use. The hipped roof of a sagging barn close by has shiny sheet metal replacing one whole section; the rest of the roof remains original shingle. Time's toll.

The baker herself delivered our croissants to the countertop and said, "Help yourself to the butter," which filled a heavy blue crock, wickedly inviting. She wore blue jeans, a dark plaid shirt, a long white apron, and a great warm smile. We were a penny short but she said that was close enough. Time's constancy. The small touches of decency don't change.

The bakery bulletin board carried hand-lettered notices of clinker-built wooden boats available at any stage of construction from framed to planked, with or without rigging. Also tacked up were the words "Shearing and crutching," accompanied by a phone number —real sheep this time, not erratic glacial boulders. We talked with Wendy Mickle about them. Young, pretty, capable, she strikes me as an ideal resident drawn to this ideal island. What do you want from today's life? What will you put into it? Wendy seems to have consciously asked the questions and to them added: What about tomorrow?

She tends a flock of ten ewes and a dozen lambs. You should speak only of breeding ewes, however, she told us. Lambs come and go, so you don't count them. "My neighbor has a mixed flock of fifty colored sheep. She'd open a shoulder fleece and say 'This one has short wool. This one, long. This one, crimpy.' So I learned about wool first and then started spinning. After that I got my own sheep."

Lopez Island has twenty to twenty-five hand spinners, two of them men. Textile arts flourish on all the San Juan Islands but Lopez concentrates on spinning and knitting, the others on weaving (though not necessarily with handspun yarn). The August county fair includes an annual sheep-to-shawl contest between islands. Four hours is allowed from shearing through carding and spinning the wool to weaving a shawl 17 x 22 inches. There are penalties if it measures a half inch over or under the specified size.

"It's nice and sociable, getting together and spinning," Wendy said. "Last month the school here suspended classes for a day and brought in community people to teach the kids spinning, dyeing, and weaving. They called me Friday for a Monday demonstration, and by phoning around I easily got the use of seven spinning wheels, even on such short notice. You can learn spinning in two or three days with a good teacher. It's not like tennis with weeks of agony."

The future? All who live in the San Juans or visit them notice the change of the last decade — a doubling of population—and all wonder what lies ahead. To translate that wondering into action, several islanders have established a San Juans land trust, which Wendy currently heads. Private, tax exempt, and nonprofit, it can accept, buy, and administer key tracts of land that contribute to the islands' unique character. A marsh here, a forested sea cliff or a threatened farmland there ... Conservation easement. Sale, with or without leaseback. Gift. The tools of the trade vary but the one goal is stewardship of the land and character of the San Juans.

"It started on Orcas in 1979," Wendy said. "The county was working on land use regulations and people suddenly realized that results are only as secure as the administration then in office. So they decided to set up a land trust that's apart from politics." Comparable trusts in the Northwest include the 40-Mile-Loop hiking and biking trail system in the city of Portland and Seattle's Evergreen Land Trust which focuses on farms and historic houses. Some trusts function around a particular issue — trails or fine old buildings. Others work to preserve the character of an area, in this case the islands.

"We've been slow getting going. There's easy agreement on the value of a 'nature bank' with tax advantages for private donors and no need to spend public dollars. But the logistics here! Even if it's only a one-hour meeting you have to catch the 7 a.m. ferry, return on the 3 p.m. ferry. We can't have evening meetings. There aren't any ferries. Everybody has to give up a whole day for each meeting.

"It's hard, too, because federal law covering easements stays confused. Congress passes something and IRS draws up applicable rules; but by then Congress may be off in a different direction. What about mineral rights, for instance? Must they go with the easement? What if you don't own them? Or want to keep those rights but donate everything else?"

Margaret Mead once commented that today's grandmothers are the first ever, anywhere, to cradle babies in their arms without knowing what patterns those beginning lives ultimately will follow. The pace of change has so quickened that it's smashed most of the templates one generation can pass to the next. Anchors no longer hold. So people seek a simpler life by moving to the San Juans and going back to raising sheep —or they at least come to visit.

"This day in history," a Canadian Broadcasting Corporation announcer intoned a bit ago and then described the last sighting in Canada of a passenger pigeon: May 18, 1903. The date is also the anniversary of Mount St. Helen's big 1980 eruption and, nearly 200 years ago, of when Lieutenant William Broughton entered the passage between Lopez and San Juan Islands in the *Chatham*. For the great mariner Captain George Vancouver and the royal British throne, Broughton "discovered" these islands — though if local Indians could have known the paleskins' thinking, they surely would have wondered how land inhabited since withdrawal of the ice sheet could suddenly be discovered by strangers so far from home.

Underway—May 19:
As we were leaving Fisherman's Bay just now, a great blue heron crossed our bow gliding only a foot above the water, long legs trailing, head so tucked to shoulders you'd never guess it has a long neck. Rhinoceros auklets flip beneath the surface, then pop back up like corks. The white facial feathers and head tufts of their breeding plumage make twin stripes. They look like carefully made-up clowns. I sit on *Taku's* bow, binoculars glued to eyes. I watch an immature bald eagle, sitting disarrayed on a rock, take sudden wing and alight in the top of a tall spruce where an eagle more classically belongs. And I watch a seal swim parallel to us, its gray head shiny-wet and held so that only the eyes are above water. Louis says it must be adding us to its life list of people sightings.

Glaucous winged gulls whiten the end of the sand spit this morning exactly as they did yesterday. They stand beyond the beached reef-net boats, which are long and narrow: canoe-like. Indeed, reef netting is an Indian fishing method that reaches who knows how far into the past. Sockeye salmon en route to the Fraser River to spawn swarm across the reefs of eastern Juan de Fuca Strait and the main channels of the San Juan and Gulf Islands. With careful ritual and great ingenuity, Salish people living along these waterways intercepted the fish and welcomed them, calling them Elder Brother and Honored Ones. First arrivals were treated to elaborate ceremony that included putting all bones back into the water so that when Salmon People returned to their village beneath the sea, they could easily reclothe themselves in flesh and come again to visit the camps of their human younger brothers.

Reef netting never was widespread. It belongs only to the San Juan Islands and to adjacent Vancouver Island from about Sooke (west of Victoria) to Saanich (the present B.C. Ferry landing), along with the mainland shores of Point Roberts and Boundary and Birch Bays. People in this one area — the Lummi, Semiahmoo, Samish, Saanich, and Songish — actually spoke a different language than other, neighboring Salish groups. Reef netting is that special. Indians knew the precise physical character of their world and the habits of every creature that swam, walked, or flew. They drew on generations-worth of learning. Among Lummis, the First Man to inhabit the world lived at the north end of San Juan Island, most likely at Garrison Bay where the Pig-War British troops camped.

Reef-net rigs consisted of two canoes with a net suspended horizontally between them. As salmon swam over the net, men raised it and emptied the silvery largesse into one of the canoes. What's remarkable? The precision of their operation, beginning with the advance preparation. The system worked only when the rig was positioned directly in the path of the migrating fish. Since salmon get a "free ride" on the tidal currents, use was restricted to the few hours of active ebbing or flooding. Nets had to be set facing the flow.

Chiefs owned the rights to specific locations and valued them highly, for daily catches ran to 2,000 or more fish from a single net under ideal conditions. Sun-dried and stored, that food surplus made a chief worthy of commoners' loyalty: he had the means to care for them. And only with commoners to fish and hunt and gather food and materials could a chief hope to make his name great.

Generally men set reef nets where kelp forests grew from gently sloping bottoms. To direct the fish, they cleared a path through the kelp stems, leading to the forward edge of the net. In deep water or on reefs that had no kelp, they often suspended a false bottom of horizontal ropes reaching forward from the net. Tufts of ryegrass tied onto the ropes helped direct the Honored Ones. No bait was used. No hooks or gill netting. Knowledge of migration routes and times sufficed to guide the salmon a bit and intercept them. Only bright, calm days offered success; and the water had to be clear enough that the fishing captain, who stood in the stern of one of the canoes, could see the fish approach. Poor weather or choppy water clouded this visibility.

When the captain saw salmon jumping close to his net, he sang out, "Thank you, Elder Brother. Come, Elder Brother." And he waved his hand up and down to startle the fish into crossing the net's forward edge. Once they'd done so and were in position above the net, he called "Lift, lift, lift, lift," and his crew pulled on lines supporting the sides of the net. As many as twelve men might work together, six to a canoe.

Anchor lines attached amidships, not at bow or stern, held the two canoes apart, and a predetermined length of slack line was looped around a thwart and held by a pin. When the captain shouted, "Let it go," crewmen pulled these pins and the canoes floated alongside each other, gunwale to gunwale. The crew closest to shore started pulling the net into their canoe, while the men opposite them slid fish off into their own canoe, ritually greeting the Swimmers.

Nets had to be made anew each year—which means that hand-spinning here dates farther back than most of today's Lopez Islanders realize. Women spun yarn for blankets from the fleece of mountain goats and of special, small dogs kept for their wool; but even more they spun endless cordage from strips of willow bark and long fibers taken from nettles (though how they harvested the nettles without getting stung always puzzles me). From the cordage men fashioned the nets, ancient forerunners of today's Sheep-to-Shawl.

No fishing rigs are in use this month. The sockeye come in July and August. From about 1890 until 1934, reef netting dwindled because the insatiable demand of canneries for salmon encouraged a faster supply of catches than old methods could produce. Salmon traps soon replaced reef nets. But their short-range efficiency so devastated the spawning runs that traps were legally banned in the mid 1930s, and reef-net captains again began watching for sockeye and directing their crews in hauling the nets.

The artist Theodore Winthrop, who canoed through the Northwest in 1853, wrote that a reef-net captain's headdress looked "like a rat's nest confected of wool, feathers, furry tails, ribbons, and rag." It's always easier to disparage than to understand, to laugh at appearances than to know meanings. The headdress was a badge of office. Of cedar bark, it included a wide brim to shade the captain's eyes and it so symbolized the coming of the Elder Brothers that within the house at night it sat prominently on a pole; it indicated that the captain was alertly watching for salmon, even when not in the canoe.

Whole crews worked together putting in anchors to hold each pair of canoes parallel to each other. Beach rocks so big they took two or more men to lift them were girdled with cedar-bough ropes and loaded onto a platform of planks laid across both canoes. Crewmen dropped over the first rock attached to the anchor line, then ten to twelve more rocks, each with a loop of rope that was threaded onto the anchorline.

Reef-net boats now are modern but still long and narrow, still paired. Towers ten to fifteen feet high lift the watchmen for a better view of the Honored Ones. Polaroid glasses instead of "rat's-nest" headgear cut the surface glare. Power winches raise the nylon nets that have replaced hand-hauled willow-bark nets; and crewmen transfer sockeye into mesh holding pens to stay fresh until the local fish buyer makes his rounds. Fundamentally, however, remarkably little has changed—except perhaps the size of the haul. A catch of 300 to 400 fish per day is now considered good, one fifth what it used to be.

Out in the open strait, you sail through an absolute maze of floats, marking the sets of gillnetters and purse seiners based at Richardson and Mackaye Bay and Friday Harbor. Only in the more intricate island waterways do you see the reef netters. It's there that currents race as fingering torrents to sweep through narrow passes and around obstructing rocks. Each turn of the tide flushes the sea first one way, then the other. The surface may be slick, the day silent; then you hear a roaring and splashing and soon ride a river of white water. Foot-high waves break and foam against the hull, swirling you through a whirlpool and close to a rocky point where seals doze in the sun. Beyond, the current will dissipate, and you'll be back in flat-calm water. These white-water sea rivers are elemental and a joy to float, providing your boat carries a fathometer to read out bottom depths and an engine to overpower the current should the need suddenly arise. Louis seeks these free rides. So do the salmon.

Rounding the south end of Lopez is my favorite sail in all of the islands—at least whenever the south end of Lopez is where we happen to be. I choose differently when we're winding through Wasp Passage at sunset, its myriad islets turned to cardboard cutouts against a flaming sky; or when we're anchoring at Matia in the dark with the lights of the ski lift at Grouse Mountain, B.C., tracing an astonishing vertical stripe of electric glitter onto an otherwise all-velvet canvas. I'm fickle about favorites. But for now, these Lopez cliffs and rocks are it.

Lopez stretches twelve miles long and four wide. Flat and rolling, it's a farming island with orchards, dairy herds, poultry, and pigs, as well as sheep. It's the island favored by most bicyclists since the terrain is so manageable. At the south end, however, wild headlands plunge straight into the sea and even close against them, the bottom registers thirty fathoms (180 feet) and more. There's no slope. Furthermore, as if unwilling to quit, the cliffs continue offshore as crags and rock islets. Currents roar and splash. Seals and killer whales, gulls and cormorants plunge and feed; fishermen set their nets and trolling lines. At this time of year spring salmon weighing eight to twenty pounds come to feed on herring fry. Earlier, blackmouths (immature kings) to thirty-five pounds swim the depths, hungry and responsive to spinner and mooching.

In 1901 a half million salmon caught here rotted. Men pulled nets so fast and full that the pickling plant ran out of both salt and barrels, and spoilage ran rampant. Nobody thought. They just fished—and failed to honor their Elder Brothers. That was a quarter century after the arrival of homesteader George Richardson and the beginning of the town named for him. The settlement boasted the first post office on Lopez Island and the first public meeting hall, a combination church and social hall (though claiming it as first disregards the far bigger longhouses of the Indians—as much as 400 feet long by 40 feet wide—which doubled as dwelling, warehouse, workshop, dance theater, church, and social hall).

Soon after the rotting-fish fiasco, Lopez was blessed with the installation of a phone system—and a chance to flaunt bureaucracy. Someone had assumed that permission for poles would be forthcoming and went ahead without waiting for the application to be stamped with official approval. Result? No sooner were the poles up than they came back down and men filled in their holes. Jurisdiction thus clarified, permission was formally granted and poles and lines went back up. Trespass never has been countenanced lightly here. Sometimes the issue is profound, as today's dilemma of how to fit public access and preferences in with private rights. Other times the matter has been totally — even flagrantly — individualistic. Settlers of George Richardson's era often claimed "citizenship of convenience." Joint occupancy by British and Americans still prevailed and considerable financial gain lay in claiming loyalty to whichever government the tax collector knocking at the door did *not* represent.

Smugglers knew a heyday. Sheep wool from Canada got mixed in with island wool and sold at American prices, double that of British North America. The arithmetic of pounds of wool purchased divided by known size of flocks, however, equated to a gloriously impossible island production per sheep. Battles raged for decades. As early as 1851, U.S. Customs inspectors had seized the Hudson's Bay Company steamer *Beaver* and attempted to collect duty, the first incident of hundreds yet to come, for at that time commerce was booming in this corner of the Northwest. Lumber shipments from Puget Sound to San Francisco flourished almost as soon as Sutter found his gold, and they continued right through the great rebuilding after the Bay City's 1906 earthquake and fire.

Port Townsend, international port of entry on the northeast corner of the Olympic Peninsula, swarmed with foreign consulates and U.S. officialdom, including Immigration and Customs. The San Juans, readily visible across the Strait of Juan de Fuca, swarmed equally with opportunists flashing coded messages and making swift dashes in small, sleek craft. Their illicit cargo? Everything from British wool and rum to opium (legal but taxed at $10 per pound beginning in 1890). Tragically, contraband also included Chinese laborers released by the thousands in 1883 following completion of the transcontinental Canadian Pacific Railroad. Excluded from legal entry into the United States, these unfortunates represented readymade opportunity for profiteering smugglers who sometimes abandoned their pitiful human cargo on a low island, giving them false promises of a nearby town; or, according to grisly, undocumented reports, even jettisoned them if a revenue cutter drew close.

Labyrinthine passages and myriad hidden coves and wooded hillsides perfect for caching goods gave smugglers an advantage in the "contest." So did the slowness of the government fleet, consisting at first of one leased private vessel and one canoe, so patently limited that Customs collectors rode aboard passenger steamers hoping to catch small-scale culprits. They also bribed Canadian informers with promises of a share of proceeds from the sale of confiscated goods. If "Smugglers Pass" and "Contraband Cove" aren't among island placenames, they should be. There is a forlorn rock islet between San Juan and Lopez Island shown on most charts as China Rock, sad reminder of a grim chapter in the history of Paradise.

Birdwatching turns me philosophical — and in these waters without turning my head, I see hundreds of marine birds of more than a dozen species. I watch a pair of auklets and note exactly how they submerge. For example: first the head goes down; then the tail makes a brief, triangular appearance; and they're gone. No thrashing with feet or wings, or squawking. The auklets are looking at you with their striped faces and yellow bills. And then they're not. I'm reminded of the Japanese ideal for life, which underlies the national admiration for cherry blossoms. Live gloriously while your moment lasts, then vanish swiftly and silently.

We circle Davidson Rock, grassy-topped, white-dotted with gulls, and accented with two coal-black crows sitting on the wildlife refuge sign. Somber gray cliffs are split by crevices whitened with cormorant droppings. Within the crack sit the nesting birds. These are the common pelagic cormorants, which fly past us with necks outstretched as though trying to catch up with their own heads. They are the species that seems to sit at every anchorage holding out wings to dry. At the tops of the cliffs here, however, silhouetted against the sky in an un-cormorant-like position, is a cluster of 100 or so other cormorants: the far less common double-crested species. We can see the scraggly stick piles of their nests, for double-crested cormorants go through motions of proper concerned parenthood, cradling eggs and young within a nest rather than laying directly onto rock and trusting to fate, which is the way of their slapdash cousins.

Drifting with motor off and sails slack we count at least eighty pelagic cormorant nests on the face of a cliff. They're easily noticed by the whitewashing from generations of droppings. We hear the birds' vocal *chgggg-ing* and *whooo-ing*. Each one arches its neck a time or two when it flies in, and gurgles thus to—or at—its mate. Sometimes we see a cormorant try to land where the cliff is too vertical: it makes one quick attempt at a touchdown, lowering its big black feet for the landing; then it thinks better of it and falls off to try again. Birds already successfully perched face inward — toward the cliff — and they brace with their broad, longish tails as if acting the part of woodpeckers on a tree trunk. White breeding patches show conspicuously on each side of the rump.

The tide stands at about the halfway point. White barnacles and brown seaweed streak the base of the cliffs, exposed to the aerial world. Without a printed schedule, you can "read" the stage of the tide by the lifeforms conspicuous wherever rocks meet sea. Assessing the tide sometimes is crucial in deciding whether to risk a passage with questionable depth below the keel or to calculate what your forward progress is likely to be. Small-boat engines may be unable to fight the current; the only choice is to go with the flow. We have no predetermined itinerary, however; we suit schedule and psyche to fit the realities.

A while back, Mount Rainier was floating above Ebey's Landing on Whidbey Island, and I remembered that before making his famous landing there in 1850 and establishing a farm, Isaac Neff Ebey had served as a U.S. Customs inspector. In that role he tried — unsuccessfully — to tax the Hudson's Bay Company farm a year before their pig got loose and wandered into history. Now the peak commanding the horizon is Mount Baker, the state's northernmost volcano. Except for its smooth pyramidal lines, it looks more like a cloud than a mountain at the moment. We notice the gleam of the Deception Pass Bridge, too, the lighting on it intensified by the sun's low angle. This is the hour to be out and savoring this Northwest. The clock says 1730 (5:30 pm) which should be cook-dinner time. But appetites had best stay flexible when afloat. Who wants to be in the galley while the great evening light show of the islands is about to begin? Allow yourself sherry and apple slices and sit in the cockpit to marvel. I'm cold but too entranced to go below for a jacket.

Suddenly Louis bursts out laughing in his delightful way. He's just remembered the allegorical man who didn't want a radio with a marine band on his boat because he hated military music. So much for solemn thoughts of ethereal beauty. ... Louis swivels the fathometer so he can see it from the tiller, and we thread the tight pass between Frost Island and Spencer Spit. Four masts jut skyward beyond the spit. That should mean eleven mooring buoys still left at the state park. We'll tie up there.

Shaw Island – May 20:

We rowed ashore at Spencer Spit this morning to empty the Porta-Potty. Hooray for the State Park System for providing the dump facility. Little loss for them. Big gain for the public, for the chore is surprisingly difficult to take care of. There's a need and a law: who wants polluted waters, especially if today's volume of boaters all pumped waste overboard? Yet there's no provision for complying with the need and law at most docks; there aren't any facilities. Not even at the National Park Service dock at Garrison Bay. They post signs there telling you not to bring garbage ashore.

We strolled out Spencer Spit. Campsites are both walk-in and drive-in, and at the very tip of the spit, perhaps half a mile from the parking lot, there are picnic tables and a log shelter built by homesteader Roy Spencer about the time of World War I. He intended it as a guest cabin. And how the "guests" have multiplied! Public use at this park has quadrupled in the last decade, rising from 11,000 in 1970 to more than 48,000 in 1976, then dropping a bit with the gasoline shortage and curtailed travel. Summer nights find fifty to seventy boats riding at anchor among the fifteen mooring buoys provided by the state park.

A van with a retired couple in it pulled up as we started out the sand spit. They asked about clamming and all we could report were plenty of squirts and bleaching shells. They grabbed shovels and a bucket and sloshed off across the lowtide flat. Their voices mixed with the cry of a lone killdeer that must have had eggs in the sedge or pickleweed edging the marsh. "Is that the kind of clam that keeps digging?" the woman's voice drifted out to us. And then, "You go on. I'll fill in holes. Oh, gee, we're going to have a good lunch."

The killdeer went into its broken-wing act, classic deception intended to lure intruders away from a nest. Then she flew close to the lapping salt water, and for a while I watched a killdeer through clam squirts. Violet-green swallows darted over the marsh and a barn swallow flew past no more than eight inches above the sand, first its rusty belly banked our way, then its glossy blue-black back. Nearby we heard a sound like that of a spoon in a plastic dish, and we watched a gull dip its yellow bill into a crab shell, feeding to the far corners. Two crows stood close, drawfed in size by the gull. I constantly think of gulls as big-pigeon size, but actually they outdo chickens, approaching about turkey length, if not weight. Our bird book lists glaucous winged gulls as twenty-two inches long.

From Spencer Spit we sailed through Harney Channel, named for General William L. Harney, the American commander who dispatched George Pickett and his troops from the frontier fort at Bellingham to San Juan Island in 1859. Place names here give a disjointed history. For instance, Grindstone Bay on the Orcas side of Harney Channel gets its name from the 1860s: Paul K. Hubbs, who operated the only store on the island, also had the only grindstone. It drew settlers rowing in from all over to sharpen their hand tools, vital for wrestling homes from the wilderness.

The name Eastsound, the village at the head of the Orcas Island inlet with Rosario Resort, became one word by Post Office decree. That would distinguish it from West Sound (two words), a community on the small, pastoral bay next westward. Government logic.

Pole Pass, leading from Harney Channel on toward the sunset, gets its name from the nets Indians strung onto poles to intercept ducks and geese flying through the narrow passage. In adjacent Wasp Passage, so far as I know, nobody ever got stung. The name is for the war sloop USS *Wasp*; and nearby Jones Island (now a state park) commemorates the ship's commander, Jacob Jones. Why? Because the peripetetic nineteenth-century Navy commander Lieutenant Charles Wilkes mapped the islands and put scores of irrelevant military names into the official record. He wanted to call Orcas Island for Commodore Isaac Hull, commander of the frigate USS *Constitution,* and to name East Sound "Old Ironside Inlet." He further proposed that West Sound be named "Guerrière Bay" after the English vessel captured by Hull off the Massachusetts coast during the War of 1812.

Fortunately, Mount Constitution is the only legacy of these particular Wilkes' names. Orcas Island kept the name given it in 1792 by the Spanish explorer Francisco Eliza who sailed by order of the Mexican viceroy, Don Juan Vincente Guemes Panchecho y Padilla Orcasites y Aguayo Conde de Revilla Gigedo. His name alone inspired "Guemes" Island and "Padilla Bay" as well as "Orcas" Island — appropriate designations commemorating civic beginnings as a Spanish outpost.

We're now docked at Shaw Landing. Tonight we're going to the "water meeting," a report to the citizenry by U.S. Geological Survey scientists who, at the request of county commissioners, have looked into the condition of the water table in these islands. The meeting will be at the school, so we expected to anchor in Blind Bay and row ashore, then walk. Glassing the bay, we saw nothing but private land: no place to beach a dinghy. Consequently we have tied up at the dock.

I walk to the little store to ask permission, but it's closed. The post office next door is open but a spirited conversation is underway across the counter and I hate to intrude. So I read the bulletin board on the porch. Notice of the water meeting is posted. Next to it is a plea from Smitty the garbage man urging everybody to put their names onto their cans and/or bags, else, "How can I know what to charge you, especially those of you that don't put out garbage very often?" Smitty adds that he's fairly new on the route and will soon be training an even newer driver for the summer, so — please — let's all cooperate.

Also posted are a predictable number of notes regarding boats and outboard motors and cords of firewood; and there's one from a California teacher wanting to house-sit or share quarters for the summer while drawing on island settings for some unspecified writing project; another concerning problems of nuclear war. I read them all; then finally interrupt the post office conversation and ask about the dock. "I have no idea," the post office lady answers, though even I could throw the proverbial stone from her stamp window to where *Taku* is tied. Still she's right. It's good judgment, especially in a small community, not to speak for your neighbor. Besides she continues: "The nuns operate the dock. Walk up the stairs and knock on their door."

So I do, and the door is opened by a stereotypically plain-but-pretty woman dressed in a long brown habit with a veil covering her hair and a heavy iron cross hanging from a chain about her neck: a Franciscan sister. Beyond her I see a dining table overlooking the Washington State Ferry slip. It's set for six, with dinner evidently imminent. I ask about staying at the dock. She charges me 20 cents per foot of *Taku's* length. I walk back to the boat and start cooking dinner. With ironic timing, the ferry arrives, and its wake bounces us about so that I'm challenged to simultaneously hold in place the wine glasses, the frypan of cooking hamburger, and the cutting board with leaf lettuce and radishes set out for a salad.

Louis stands on the dock taking a picture of the ferry, and passengers aboard it line the railing to take pictures of *Taku*. "Look out the window," Louis calls, and I catch a glimpse of the sister from whom I rented the dock space. She's turning the crank that raises the ferry-slip gangplank. The dock's pilings put her high above our level; we see her as an improbable silhouette of flowing robes and veil backdropped by five cars driving off the ferry.

Tomorrow the store will be open and I'll ask more.

Yellow Island – May 21:
The Franciscan nuns operate the Shaw Landing general store, as well as the dock and ferry slip. And what a store it is! Frozen foods, wines, cheeses, beautiful fattening pastry including huge cinnamon twists I thought must be from Holly B's Bakery on Lopez but which turn out to come from Bellingham. The store is called the Little Portion, named after Saint Francis of Assisi's chapel in Italy. I pressed for some connection between the two, but a radiantly smiling gray-haired nun answered only that this island seems a little portion of the coast and the landing a little portion of the island.

Next I asked if their order has other commercial endeavors. She responded that their mission is to serve and that five years ago this store and the dock needed someone to operate them. One of the sisters who comes on weekends from Bellingham is a licensed mortician. Another teaches music at the Shaw Island school and also gives private lessons; her San Pietro Music Studio is in the warehouse at the end of the ferry dock. Next to it is the Mother Kepper Chapel, and across from the two, also on the dock, is a small greenhouse with geraniums blooming and hanging baskets with fuchsias and lobelias that promise future glory.

At the store's checkout counter a young couple ahead of us in line — obviously bicyclists — were purchasing the two largest cans of beer I've ever seen. The nun waiting on them held up one of the cans and summoned a second sister who was busy stocking shelves. We glanced at the young people, assuming their age was under scrutiny. But the approaching sister simply remarked on their good taste in beer. She's from Australia, and whenever customers pick Australian beer, she likes to congratulate them, the nun at the cash register explained. Her statement also explained our confusion a moment ago. The Australian nun had noticed our juggling more unexpected purchases than hands could comfortably hold, and she'd gently commented: "May I suggest you take a trolley?" Now we realize that's Australian for "shopping cart."

After dinner Louis and I walked to the water meeting — or got about halfway there when a Volkswagen beetle passed us, backed, and picked us up. The driver was Judy, the post office lady. She's been on the island three years and reports that 130 people live here now with three more houses going up. Increasing residents and "especially the week-enders" are having real impact. (A fashionably overworked word is "impact"; it says nothing about what's happening.)

The school, a frame one-room building listed on the National Register of Historic Places, radiates tending and love. Present enrollment totals eight elementary pupils. High school students cross to Orcas or board in Anacortes. They used to row both ways across Harney Channel in a skiff "with only five inches of freeboard when the S'easter was blowing, but they always made it," one of the old-timers at the meeting told me admiringly. Kitty-corner across the crossroads from the school is the Shaw Island Museum, a log cabin set in a mossy, fern-carpeted forest with a reef-net rig out in front of the building. "Interesting to visit even when closed," I remember a guide book commenting about this museum. We of course added it to our list of museums we've not entered.

Only fourteen people attended the meeting, plus two men from the County Planning Commission and three from the USGS. Arriving early, we'd helped Judy haul folding chairs for forty from the basement storage cave under the schoolroom. So much for rural-community involvement in their own fate: but who among us welcomes adding facts to feelings?

The water issue in the San Juans is attended by considerable emotion. "Island Water: A problem that's too hot to handle," the *Island Record* heralded a couple of weeks ago. "When Steve Swanberg goes to get ice cubes, he invariably finds a salt lick in the bottom of the tray. He has a problem that is shared by a disturbing number of residents: salt water intrusion in his well."

Swanberg lives on San Juan just west of where Hudson's Bay Company kept their pigs. His water comes from a well that serves nine houses, five of them "fulltime," the island term for houses lived in year round. Another twenty-nine houses are to be served by that same well, though the lots for several of these haven't yet been sold. The well, near the shoreline, reaches 100 feet below sea level. Swanberg is reported as feeling that by the time the houses of the second county-approved plat are built "that well will be drawing straight salt water." Yet the sign advertising Eagle Cove Estates Division II carries no whisper of warning. It simply says: "All utilities in, including a new state-approved water system."

State standards allow 250 milligrams of chloride per liter of water, an amount somewhere below a clearly salty taste but approaching a problem level for heart patients and others. Until that degree of contamination is reached, or exceeded, no violation has occurred. But once salt water has entered an aquifer, just try to get it out. Checks of sixty wells on the four islands served by ferries showed that most of them are drilled to below sea level, and ten percent already are suffering salt-water intrusion. Furthermore, this is happening while the water rights in actual use represent less than one-fifth of those that have been allocated. Land developments must have a water source before they're platted; but who can guarantee the ongoing volume of that source? There are instances of wells producing eight gallons a minute, then dropping to a trickle a year later.

Sailing the San Juans, you're aware that no waterfalls leap from cliffs and few creek mouths pour fresh water into salt, as so typifies cruising elsewhere in the Northwest. The 8,000-foot Olympic Mountains bounding the island realm to the south are responsible for this. They so effectively wring the wet legacy from clouds sweeping in from the Pacific that little rain is left to moisten the San Juan Islands. The average is only about two feet per year, so little it would terrify every slug in the Rain Forest, a scant sixty miles away on the west side of the Olympic Peninsula. Yearly rainfall there is about sixteen feet.

Water flowing from present day island wells is "fossil water" soaked down to subterranean aquifers through the long millennia since the melting of the last glacier ice. Current replenishment can't keep pace with withdrawals. Consequently pressure from surrounding sea water diffuses salts into the freshwater lenses. Water is most abundant where glacial gravels cover the islands, such as on Lopez, much of San Juan, and the Eastsound region of Orcas Island. On solid bedrock islands like Shaw, water collects in cracks and faults, and success in drilling a long-lasting well largely depends on hitting a bountiful crack.

"What's the answer?" people asked after the geologists had shown their slides and given their data. But planning, of course, must come from the local level, not the federal. The USGS team offered no solutions. Their dispassionate notice is that short-range attitudes may carry long-range consequences.

"What about cisterns?" someone asked. And another member of the miniscule audience answered that a month-and-a-half worth of rain collected off a roof in a cistern produced 92,000 gallons of water. People pointed to Frank Richardson, a retired University of Washington professor friend of ours who lives near Deer Harbor on Orcas and uses only cistern water. "Yes," someone sighed, "but whenever Frank comes to visit, he asks to take a shower."

Everybody laughed, and the Shaw Island water meeting adjourned. Louis and I walked the two-and-a-half miles back to the dock so as to watch the last of day merge with the beginning of night. Five or six deer watched us from a field, and we noticed that people living in the house at the field's edge had ringed their garden with a six-foot fence, needed as protection against deer. The does watching us set off stiff-legged, as if they were mechanical toys with overwound springs. They cleared three-strand barbed wire without pausing—a beautiful, leaping ballet silhouetted in the dimming light with a backdrop of rosy sky and polished water. Across the road from the deer's field we passed a split-rail fence still structurally intact but so overgrown with wildrose and Douglas-fir saplings that we wouldn't have seen it except for being afoot.

On the beach at Blind Bay lay three or four rotting reef-net boats and in an adjacent field we counted an additional fifteen or so, long abandoned. An unseen peacock shouted its eerie call from somewhere in the gloaming, and frogs croaked boisterously. A heron stood in the water more than knee deep so that the merest strip of water separated its real self from its inverted, reflected self. It waited till we had passed and actually were getting farther away; then it flew silently. A grebe floated close to shore, also double until it arched its slender neck and vanished into its own reflection.

We anchored here once last summer. It was a cold dark Saturday night at the crowded height of the season, and we dreaded the hassle of a full dock or state park cove. Barely through Harney Channel, Louis spotted a small ketch he'd always admired during the time we used to launch our sloop at Horsehead Bay, near Tacoma. The boat turned in here, and we followed. It sought the lee of the forested east shore where other boats already were anchored; but we wanted privacy, so headed straight for a dozen Herefords and Charolais grazing at water's edge with a pasture and an orchard behind them. Louis meant to pull close to shore to minimize effects from the wind blowing across the low farmland; but a utility raft was moored between our position and shore, and on it were fifteen to twenty cormorants drying their wings. We couldn't upset the scene of peaceful cows and peaceful cormorants, so we dropped anchor farther out.

Perhaps thirty boats were in the bay that night, two thirds of them sailboats (mostly from Canada), the rest commercial trawlers. Lights from Orcas shone across the channel, making that village look ten times its actual wee size. A time or two the ferry churned purposefully past, its waves spent without even rippling the bay. Human voices rarely rose audibly, despite the high number of boats; and the only people using motors were locals pulling crab pots.

We're now at Yellow Island, a small romantic stitch within the islands' tapestry. Yellow lies west of Wasp Passage, a low island of a scant eleven acres now owned by The Nature Conservancy but previously the kingdom of Lew and Tib Dodd. Lew sailed on clipper ships, then married Tib, and for twenty years the two farmed on Orcas. In 1947 they retired to Yellow Island

Time weathers buildings at landings where old patterns of use no longer are valid.

Maintaining a classic wooden boat guarantees a peculiar satisfaction—and an answer for anybody wondering how to spend time, money, and effort.

and lived in a tent while building a driftwood cabin. That took two years. Lew Dodd died in 1960, yet everywhere you look he seems gently present.

The cabin, 27x35 feet, has only one room but in its way is a palace as gracious as Robert Moran's. True, the Rosario music room alone would swallow the Dodd mansion, but I doubt that either the Morans or the Dodds believed that size alone measured quality or craftsmanship or love. Moran arrived in Seattle from the East with less than the cost of a hotel room in his pockets and from that beginning climbed the classic American ladder to wealth and social standing. He built with what he had at hand, which was money. The result embodies the splendor of gleaming white plaster on the outside with imported, hard carved wood, sumptuous carpeting, and stained glass windows to enjoy while inside. The Morans lived genuinely in their way. So did the Dodds.

What Lew and Tib had available was flotsam brought by the currents, and little money. They had patience, a quality the Morans perhaps couldn't afford when they started to build, for before he moved to Orcas, doctors had begun a countdown on Robert Moran's life.

Louis and I sit now in the Dodd palace talking with Dr. David Duggins and Dr. Megan Dethier, husband-and-wife researchers at the University of Washington Friday Harbor Labs. Young, brilliant, and strong-but-gentle, David and Megan are the ideal successors of Lew and Tib Dodd. They live in the cabin and love and manage the island for The Nature Conservancy. Megan lifts lasagne from the wood-range oven and dishes out salad tossed from the bounty of the fish-net enclosed garden beyond the window. We feast and talk.

The cabin is low—even I must duck to clear the door lintel—and windows are set close to the ground so that you can see out while seated within. "He built his way and for his height, which was five feet two inches," David comments. All materials are salvage; the sea served as deliveryman, and yet there's a consistency of style that came from the Dodds' patient waiting for the quality they required. They stayed wonderfully flexible in their planning rather than holding blindly to some predetermination. The Dodds lived *with* their island, not just on it.

Their hearth is bedrock: the island itself incorporated into one corner of the cabin. Natural cracks are filled with pebbles held by concrete; the chimney is built of stones from the beach. Cabin walls are driftwood logs set upright, some with bark still on. Ship hatch-covers provide flooring and Dutch doors. A brass porthole serves as window in the top half of the front door, typical of the workmanship here — for think of hand-fitting a heavy round brass frame into a hole cut through the planks of a hatch cover. An edging of rope trims the porthole. Rope also trims the windows and the book shelves which divide living area from sleeping area.

David and Megan commute to work by Zodiac, twenty minutes in a fast rubber boat on calm summer days, half-an-hour in winter — "or an hour-and-a-half, or never; it's a great way to start the day." Certainly the commute takes the two beyond mere theoretical investigation of their research into hearty daily participation: seabirds and porpoises and killer whales are more than paragraphs on a page. Once they even passed a bull elephant seal asleep in mid channel. "He looked soooo big from the Zodiac," Megan says. Lummi In-

dians used to claim that you could locate lone elephant seals by their loud snoring, but that to spear one you first had to lift its bulbous trunk off its chest. They called these two-ton bulls "sleepers" and called people who slept so soundly they lost awareness of surroundings by the same word as that for elephant seal.

What land animals live on Yellow Island? we ask. "Mink," Megan answers. "Also river otters, which feed mostly on crabs and fish, and I've even seen one eating a seabird. There are raccoons, too. Once we trapped a female raccoon and took her to Shaw Island, but she practically beat us back here to Yellow. She had to swim Wasp Passage, and the currents there are ferocious! Later we found she had four kits so young she still was keeping them hidden. They were in an abandoned crow nest well draped with honeysuckle vines. A little movement there caught my eye one day, and up peeked a tiny furry head.

"Deer swim to the island too, especially does about to give birth. Small outlying islands are safer for fawns because predators are few. We have twin fawns here now. But three deer on an eleven-acre island is 2.9 too many. They eat too high a percentage of plants' green shoots."

Yellow Island is maintained as a wildflower preserve. The Nature Conservancy, a private land trust, bought it in 1980 because the island protects a rich and varied assemblage of flowers, largely disrupted elsewhere. Logging, farming, and grazing inevitably have taken a toll of native plants even in the San Juans. But a wide range of growing conditions, including thin soil and low rainfall, still fosters both common species and also several that are unknown in the rest of soggy western Washington. Isolated dots on the map, such as Yellow Island, are rare garden treasures. When we were on Lopez, Wendy Mickle had said: "Last April I saw more kinds of flowers out on Yellow than I'd seen cumulatively the whole rest of my life. I looked them up in flower books and found that several supposedly grow only east of the Cascades. It's really special habitat on that little island."

Purple salsify tower above vetch. Camas shoots lift their purple, lily-blossoms literally hip high, twice as tall as I've previously seen. Crimson paintbrush, sulfur-yellow lomatium, lavendar sea blush, lupine as blue as Texas bluebonnets, brown chocolate lilies, white fawn lilies, purple shooting stars . . . . Name your favorite and it's here. Prickly-pear cactus nestle in rock crevices, their fleshy pads fat as though this fundamentally desert plant finds island living surprisingly moist and easy. Shaggy-barked juniper trees — another dry-land species — also flourish. Grasses are native.

Cheat grass never got started here, which testifies to the Dodds' sensitivity. They never let the island's natural carpet grow threadbare from trampling or fire. Cheat grass indicates abused land. So do riotous growths of thistle or wildrose, or acres of bracken fern. None of these opportunists has conquered Yellow Island. Snowberry and Douglas-fir seedlings do constantly try to invade the flower meadows, but David and Megan grub them out, restricting forest to the broad middle of the island and keeping the meadows on each end open and flower-filled.

What real value have pockets of beauty and diversity like this small island? One answer lies with the thousand or so people who come here each year to enjoy the flowers, respectfully following the paths rather than crisscrossing and ruining the land, helping hold human effect to a minimum by complying with The Nature Conservancy's no-picnicking, no-camping regulations.

Beyond enjoyment, is there value? Yes. The sheer protection of diverse genes has merit that we're only beginning to realize as a society. *Harvard Magazine* recently asked: "What is the most important problem facing this nation or the world [in this decade] and what resolutions should we be making to deal with it?" The renowned Harvard sociobiologist Edward O. Wilson answered the question by beginning: "Permit me to rephrase the question as follows: What event will our descendants most regret, even those living a thousand years from now?" His answer: Not energy depletion or economic collapse. Not even limited nuclear war (if such limitation exists). "As terrible as these catastrophes would be for us," Dr. Wilson comments soberly, "they can be repaired within a few generations. The one process ongoing in the 1980s that will take millions of years to correct is the loss of genetic and species diversity by the destruction of natural habitat. This is the folly our descendants are least likely to forgive us."

We're now at nearly three species lost each day and the pace is such that by 1990 we may be losing thirty per day. Who cares? Remember when a mold with a name few of us could pronounce gave birth to penicillin? Until budget cutoffs, the National Cancer Institute worked with extracts from more than 500 species of marine invertebrates equally unknown to most of us; but snails and other mollusks don't get cancer and their immune system may someday become ours. Or there's jojoba, a desert shrub that yields oil as fine as that taken from sperm whales; and spurges and milkweeds that produce latexes so rich with hydrocarbons that the Japanese now are experimenting with plantations and expect soon to grow five to ten barrels of oil per acre per year.

What ties oil and cancer to one small island in the San Juan archipelago? The wisdom of protecting genetic diversity. It's a matter partly aesthetic and partly philosophical, since who knowingly can play God and decree life for some species, death for others? It's also a question of ecological strength, since the more kinds of genes there are, the better the odds that some will thrive despite assaults. Additionally at issue are incalculable human benefits. Nobody can say which microbe or bush or beast may hold a key to future well being for our own, absolutely bar-none, all-out favorite species: us.

Extinction is the ultimate finality. "It's even worse than book-burning," says James L. Buckley, United States Undersecretary of State for Science, "because many of the 'books' haven't yet been deciphered."

Matia Island State Park — May 22:

This morning we sailed around Waldron, the "hippy island" of the San Juans, so-called for the determined subsistence lifestyle of residents. No ferry serves the island, and no telephone line or electric power system ties it to the outside world — though one woman in her eighties, part Indian, part Finnish, who was born and raised here is said to yearn for Bonneville power. She has both propane and a generator. Her house is bright with lights and noisy with television, but her neighbors find the sound of the generator bothersome. A few other

Waldron landowners treasure money more than peace, in the view of the majority, and these few seek to enlarge the airport, build a shooting club, and sell small land parcels for fly-in weekends by city people eager to return to nature conveniently and comfortably.

To be self-sustaining takes either work or money and most Waldronites embrace the former regardless of their supply of the latter. Theirs is a hold-out island of only four-and-one half square miles where people cling more tenaciously than on other San Juan islands to the patterns of the past. Or, more correctly stated, Waldron has reverted, for it too has seen change. Ask those whose Lummi grandmothers dug camas bulbs there, or the Semiahmoos who claimed tiny, nearby Skipjack and Bare Islands: when settlers homesteaded mainland prairies that had served generations of Indian people as root gardens, the islands became the last resort for this fundamental food and festivity. Or, talk with someone like the old lady wishing for public power. She can remember when regular steamer service linked Waldron with Bellingham, thirty miles distant. The island's population then was triple its present figure of about 100 year-round residents. As recently as 1970 there were only fifteen full-timers. Today the school alone has twenty-three pupils and two teachers.

For a while a Waldron fish trap provided a front for illicit drug running. And in the early 1900s, thoroughly legitimate quarrymen cut blocks of sandstone from 580-foot Point Disney to pave streets in Tacoma and Seattle (including Yesler Way) and to tow by barge to the Columbia River mouth for use in building the jetty (or, by some reports, to tow to Aberdeen-Hoquiam for the Grays Harbor jetty).

Five steam donkeys and a crew of 100 to 150 men, mostly young Scandanavian bachelors, drilled and blasted the cliff, cutting stone into blocks 6x6x12 inches. They were among the best paid workers in the West: $1.50 an hour. The bubble of fortune popped when concrete superseded sandstone as a paving material and orders ceased. Today the profile of Point Disney stands forever altered. Moreover, it still is riddled with "coyote holes" three feet square and sixty feet deep. They're where men, gunnysacks over their boots to prevent sparks, formerly placed black powder and strung long fuses to blast free the high-grade sandstone. Steel rods that supported a catwalk around the base of the nearly vertical cliff also are still in place. You can see them from the water. Indeed, Waldron is an island best enjoyed from the water. Anchorages are poor, public land non-existent, and entry distasteful where people hold so earnestly to privacy. Waldron acts as a "gene pool" of the psyche, as Nature Conservancy lands safeguard physical gene pools of flora and fauna.

Sailing toward Matia Island, we hear CBC radio reports that the Maritime Museum in Vancouver has bid successfully in London for Captain George Vancouver's brass chronometer. Its use allowed him to measure longitude and thus to determine his position at sea, a fairly new technique at the time. Captain Vancouver used the instrument to chart the Falkland Islands before coming to the Northwest Coast, according to one report. A different version claims the careful manufacturing of the instrument took so long that Vancouver sailed without it, and the supply ship *Daedalus* brought it to him. It was at Nootka that the supply captain turned it over: the harbor on the west coast of Vancouver Island where Spaniards had built a fort and where Vancouver in 1792 successfully negotiated with their diplomats for a Spanish pullback to the California border.

In any case, the chronometer lay within the warrens of the British Museum for most of the last two centuries and now Christie's has auctioned it: 80,000 Canadian dollars will return it to this coast. I leaf pages in the copy of Vancouver's log we have aboard *Taku* and find that yesterday was the anniversary of Lieutenant Broughton and his men having drifted onto rocks along the shore of Orcas, losing their lead line (used for sounding water depth). Today's anniversary is of their exploration on Cypress Island (misnamed for its juniper trees which they took to be cypress; Eliza earlier had named the island San Vincente, another commemoration of the Mexican viceroy). Broughton's men also rowed to the beach of the tiny island off Cypress's west shore and feasted on berries, properly placing Strawberry Island onto the chart.

We circle Matia. Off its east end is Puffin Island, a colorful dot with emerald grass, blue-purple camas, rosy sea blush, white chickweed, and something yellow: flowers abundant enough to identify with binoculars (except for the something yellow). Gulls are scattered across the green. Some are mating, the males flapping their wings and shrieking the whole while. A few sit in wind-flagged trees as though trying to be eagles.

Twenty or more seals lie on the rock reef off the end of Puffin Island with a triangular navigation marker towering above them. They are fat and sleek: silvery forms that shine in the sunlight, one end with an oddly flat head, the other with flippers neatly clapped together like the hands of an obedient child clasped in prayer. Between the two ends, all is big round belly. Whenever one arches its back to raise its spotted head and look at us, its belly gets even rounder. A few seals are in the water. They paddle high, lifting shoulders above the surface to view us from a new angle. Then they slip below, doubtless to inspect *Taku's* hull from that perspective. Beyond the seals we see the towers and domes and huge gas flare of the Cherry Point oil refinery.

I dig out a book and read about Matia. In 1875 it became a lighthouse reserve but no light ever got built. Now it's a wildlife refuge and state park. For thirty years a Wisconsin Civil War veteran named Elvin H. Smith lived alone on Matia. He cleared five acres at the east end, planted a garden, raised ducks, chickens, and sheep, kept a dog and a cat as pets, and took fish from a net strung across the entrance to his cove. Every Saturday he'd row the two-and-a-half miles to Orcas and walk to Eastsound, another two miles, for supplies and socializing. He had no dock on Matia so the weekly mail boat couldn't stop, but the ship's captain would toot the whistle when he had letters. Smith then would row out. That happened almost weekly, for the hermit of Matia operated a mail order faith healing practice. He prayed for those who wrote him, and letters — some with money enclosed — frequently came from all across the country.

At age eighty-six, Elvin Smith vanished in a storm while rowing home from Orcas, his boat filled with supplies and riding leaden in the water. That was in 1921, the same year that the Legislature passed the state park act and that our friend Herb visited Robert Moran in his Rosario mansion. Moran *gave* 3,600 acres to the state for the park — 200 times the acreage that had been Smith's whole Matia domain. On Orcas, a stone marking an empty grave now memorializes Elvin Smith.

We tie up at the Matia State Park dock and have the island to ourselves. The north side is like the wet, western Washington we know and love. Sword fern grows waist high beneath hemlock. Devil's club spreads its irritant-tipped thorns. Douglas-fir trunks three to four feet through are pocked with the rectangular holes of pileated woodpeckers. Slugs bigger than a man's biggest finger slither over rotting logs, some a lovely velvety black, most the rotting-banana color I suppose gives them their name.

We find Captain Smith's cove and the moldering remnants of his handiwork. There's a root cellar dug partway into a hillside and built up with stones (mostly pieces of granite brought to Matia by the ice-age glacier). Toward the beach from it, the cabin ruins lie in the brush, one wall fallen over intact. On the point beyond this cove, we find additional human remnants. chiefly a stone hearth and English ivy climbing high into the trees. Louis says fishermen must have camped here seasonally. I think ivy suggests the year-round hopes of a woman, and I walk on watching for daffodils. A Swainson's thrush sings somewhere in the forest understory, the loveliest soloist of the Northwest, here offering a requiem.

Friday Harbor — May 23:

We tie to the municipal dock along with fishing boats and early-season pleasure boats: *Costa Plenty, Mama's Mink.* Louis remarks that boat names shouldn't comment on life or personal finances as if they were bumper stickers. Neither should they be misspellings: *C-Sprite* or *Why Knot. Taku* is the name of an Alaskan inlet that's a favorite of ours. The word means "Place Where the Wild Geese Land" in the Tlingit Indian language. In Japanese the same word means "indefatigable", "press-on."

I indulge myself in all-day conversation with people in Friday Harbor. First is Sam Buck — jolly, outgoing, the sort of man sure to turn up at Rotary Club each week. He's a realtor with native roots in these islands. His father homesteaded on Orcas. His sister was born there with an Indian midwife in attendance, "a little out of character for my mother," he comments. "Mama was a city girl raised in Philadelphia. She'd worked for Curtis Publishing Company and sung with the opera. Dad was an attorney. When a bunch of Masons found that out, they moved him over here to San Juan bodily in the early 1920s and made him prosecuting attorney. He served in the Legislature too.

"These are unique islands with unique people. My high school graduating class had eighteen kids, and sixteen went on to college. Today people everywhere are trying to find themselves — or lose themselves. I'm not such which. The character of these islands attracts them, and we end up with locals versus newcomers. Island people — longtime locals — don't like any control. We have trouble fathoming why it's necessary. Also, we're very frugal and don't like what a lot of government is costing. It's not just the new county use plan, it's the bureaucracy of all government. We're small enough here to talk to each other and work things

29

out without a lot of regulation. A lot of old-timers have nothing but their land; they need to sell.

"Water? Well, I'm sure there's a finite amount. It's a matter of using it correctly. I have a geologist working for me. He's had a lot of experience in the Orient, and he says that if we handle the water falling on our roofs we'll get by very well. There's about twenty-five inches of rain a year. Once we all used that water before public distribution systems went in. My mother stored rain water because it's soft and she liked it for washing her hair and fine undies.

"There's plenty of water on this island. Some subdivisions try to restrict water use to domestic purposes only. They don't want people to get carried away and waste water. It's hard for Seattlites moving here, they're used to having so much water. Californians are more careful. They're used to paying more for water.

"It's ridiculous to stick your head in the sand and think people won't come here. That's like closing the graveyard. Growth is as inevitable as death and taxes. They say that the population has doubled in the last decade, but what's the doubling mean? There were more people here when I was a kid than till about five years ago. Nobody really knows how many are there. They come and go — own a residence but don't stay year-round.

"Real estate activity has slowed, what with the county's land use planning and the general economy. But quality areas are still viable. Pre-retirees are buying now to retire here later. Most of us working on planning are trying to legislate good taste; but we still don't have it. There are still tin buildings and mobile homes. We get customers that see something, say, in the Denver newspaper and fly in. They ask: 'What's the controversy? There isn't any crowding here.'

"I'm like the rest of the folks: when a new house goes up where I can see it, I don't like it. But a lot of people do like to have company; there's a reason for these developments. People want a sense of community. I like open space, myself. And Carefree, my development on the west side of this island, will be half open space. There'll be separate houses and common-wall development for both families and retirees: cluster development for maybe 800 people. We're in the environmental-impact-statement stage on that right now. I've put in a lake, and it's getting 108-million gallons a year; it's running into the ocean, there's so much water from springs and rain. We can have a sewer system and central water, fire control .... Carefree shows what can be done. It's where there was an old lime quarry and, really, it's been a mess for years.

"There's no danger of our turning into an LA. There's no employment in these islands, just beauty. We don't promote. The islands promote themselves. We thought planners would assist and make it easier, not stand in the way with a superior attitude and say 'We're taking care of the land for you.' Some of that is necessary but local people are bitter. We don't like regulation."

Next I walk to the office of Ray Sheffer, county sheriff —a tall, big-boned man, the epitome of sheriff-ness, as though hired through Central Casting. "Ours is the only agency in the county geared for emergencies," he says. "In Mount Vernon you can holler HELP and get it quick. Here, we have to make-do by ourselves.

"Something like the annual jazz festival really draws too much of a crowd for us to handle, though so far there's not been a problem. Most of the people come for a family outing, but some think of Friday Harbor as an open town during that period and we just have to adjust our tolerances. We can't hire twenty-five people for three days; where'd we get them from? And you can't just hand out a badge and authority. We're used to problems though: our kind of logistics and the high cost of transporting deputies and offenders make a ouija board out of budgeting. We live with it.

"A lot of our visitors come here to bicycle — organized groups of fifty or more; family units. It's a compliment to the locals that there haven't been any accidents reported. Drivers just stay patient for four or five months and know they have to be alert on hills because there may be bicyclists on the other side. It's economically impossible for this county to put in bike lanes. The tax base won't even support repairing the existing roads.

"We are getting moped accidents. There's no license required, yet those are motor vehicles. They don't handle like a bike and if people are inattentive for just a moment — or panic — they're in an accident. I came here from the Las Vegas police department fifteen years ago. Why? Well, just look at it! It's beautiful here."

"Let's not Californicate our precious islands," I read in a Letters-to-the-Editor column of the local paper. From that opening the writer goes on to comment that LA County Commissioners apparently felt they should be able to soar with any prevailing wind, "even if it meant dividing land into small pieces and selling it to developers and promoters."

I leaf through back issues of the paper. One letter writer claims there are presently five types of residents in the islands: 1) Old-timers. 2) Dropouts, in their thirties when they sought more peaceful pastures and came here, but now nearing their fifties. Many within this group are well educated, including some with Ph.D. degrees. They're part of the back-to-the-earth and crafts movements. 3) Retirement hothouse flowers who psychologically seek "islandness" as release from city pressures but, once here, watch the boats and the whales without stirring from their verandas. They have big money and big houses. They've paid their dues to society and now sit back and draw dividends. They're used to municipal services and civic amenities. Some adjust to not having them; others sell and move on.

4) Another type of retirement people have been longtime summer residents loving the islands and the island-lifeway for years. They don't want any massive overhauls. 5) Quick-buck hopefuls who have land and naive trust in fast-talkers who urge them to subdivide.

There's Eagle Cove, this writer points out: thirty-six lots, half-a-dozen homes, and the water already at the maximum salt content allowed by state health standards. Any shore development is likely to drill below sea level and get saltwater intruding into the well. "If you think the county's Comprehensive-Plan Wars were bad, just wait for the Water Wars," this person concludes. "Thousands of dollars paid; people expecting to retire here; their water system already failing; covenants for open space overturned by sixty-percent vote within cluster developments. Neighbor will turn against neighbor then, and it will all come back on the county."

Next stop: the County Planning Department. I talk

Life on the islands gives one a chance to sit in the morning sunshine savoring coffee and neighborly companionship.

Most tourists and residents travel from island to island by ferry. The vessels' arrival and departure becomes the pulse of days spent in the San Juans.

with David Sherrard: young, professional, with previous experience in Walla Walla County. "Say that you own 200 acres of farmland and want to subdivide. Your land is zoned R-20, which means a maximum density of one dwelling per twenty acres," he says. "But dividing the whole acreage into equal-sized lots would just cut the land into a checkerboard. None of the parcels would be economical to farm. So the Comprehensive Plan requires clustering. You can transfer the residential density for the whole acreage to just a part of it, and thereby concentrate development in one agriculturally nonproductive part of the land. That preserves farming and still lets you get the theoretical sub-division value for your acreage.

"There are tax breaks if you want to commit farmland, or forestry land, to open space. That's a state program. Or you can donate the development potential to the private, nonprofit San Juan Land Trust in exchange for a conservation easement. That has tax advantages too. Either way, you can develop part of the land and leave the rest 'as is.'

"The local paper, the *Island Record,* recently ran an article by Russ Rasmussen, who farms about 1,400 acres on San Juan Island. He points out that most farming in the county is now done through leasing, not by owning the land. You read about problems of keeping farmland in active production, but shipping costs actually are pretty well in line with those elsewhere these days. Needing a ferry still means it takes longer to get produce to Seattle than from the Skagit Valley, for example. But freight costs are reasonable. Conventional wisdom claims that farming fell off in the islands because of competition from large, irrigated land east of the Cascades: the railroads gave those farmers good rates so they captured the market from island pears and apples and cabbages and strawberries. Maybe that *was* true but it's not the whole reason for farm decline today. People worry about keeping the rural character of this county with good reason, but, according to Rasmussen, railroads elsewhere aren't the problem.

"He says one reason we've lost agricultural land is because in the 1950s the federal government paid farmers to set aside acres in a land bank; paid them *not* to farm. During that time buildings and equipment weren't kept in order, and the land itself wasn't taken care of either — fences and drainage systems, things like that. In the 1960s, the land-bank program ended. By then, the acreages had deteriorated for farming, and anyway, land prices had started to boom, so there was some selling.

"Really, there are two ways to preserve farming and the pastoral, rural, scenic value: regulation and market intervention. Clustering permits development income, yet protects continued agriculture and open space. Or, sometimes government can buy land and lease it back to farmers. Or development rights can be bought or transferred without the actual development ever taking place—though this calls for real commitment of public funds. Any of these ways lets the owner get at least some of the market value of his land, while farming continues on the most productive part of it. Planning really is a way of coping with growth."

From the Planning Office I stepped down the hall to talk with Eleanor Howard, County Commissioner. She's the first female Democrat ever to run for office in this county, and the first Democrat in thirty years to penetrate the traditional Republican bastion of county politics. Gray-haired, vigorous, and feminine with a quick and warm smile, Commissioner Howard radiates earnest competence: "I got involved in community activity a few years ago by serving on the Planning Commission. There was a comprehensive plan, but basically it was an 'outside' production. So islanders didn't really accept it. Only Shaw Island voted on it favorably. The county never officially adopted it; consequently the Board of County Commissioners asked us to come up with a new plan.

"Since not enough island people had been involved in producing the first plan, we decided to divide the county into neighborhoods with similar activities and similar likelihood of future growth. Then those of us on the Planning Commission went to each group and told them, 'We don't have a plan yet, but this is what we see as needed. What do you see?' Every group had its own chairman and recorder, and some met five or six times to work out their recommendations. We asked them to look at neighborhood, district, and county as a whole: How do you want each level to be fifty years from now?

"We got the reports and combined those of each district, then checked compilations with the groups. Some said: 'You got it; that's exactly what we want.' Others said: 'No way! You have it all wrong. *This* is what we want ....' In general, people agreed they wanted to keep our special quality of life, our rural and natural areas and our feeling of open space. We combined that overall feeling with what each neighborhood had recommended and the known capabilities of the land. Then we designated permissable densities, from suburban to agricultural/timber. It's been controversial right from the beginning. Still is.

"On all major issues we county commissioners go to the individual districts to hold meetings. It's easier for the three of us to travel to Orcas or Lopez or San Juan than for the citizenry to come to the courthouse. Still, not many people come to these meetings. Sometimes it's lonely being there; we don't hear from people till they're unhappy. That's my biggest disappointment in office. The neighborhood meetings for the Comprehensive Plan were different: we structured them so that we would get people's thinking. But take the USGS study today. We're learning things we already suspected, and also things we hadn't guessed. Thin soil. Saltwater intrusion, which is much more common than we realized. Land that doesn't perk. Or if it does, it's the same place that the water is coming from, so we're getting high bacteria counts in our wells. Contamination. Not many people turn out to hear about it. I guess problems have to be personal before people recognize much meaning.

"When growth began in this county, it was hard to make a living here. Then the selling began, and there were new jobs and businesses. People could have amenities and enjoy some entertainment they never had before, like the annual visit of the Seattle Symphony. For old-timers, life has gotten better. They're not the ones who want to close the gate now. Some of them recognize that there are problems, but they also worry about too many regulations. It used to be they could walk anywhere, hunt anywhere, fish anywhere. And now they miss that.

"New-timers tend to be more protective than old-timers. They don't remember how it used to be but now they worry about how it's becoming. You see this open land. It's still here. But we've *got* to find the extent of the threats to it and say, 'This is all we can bear. This is the saturation point.' We have to find that way *before* we run out of our liveable land. It's a beautiful, beautiful county."

Roche Harbor—May 24:

A pigeon guillemot leaps from the water on our port side and flies to join a friend to starboard. The two paddle away, red feet showing just a bit. Both peck at the water, nervously tossing drops aside. The red linings of their throats exactly match their feet.

Louis set a compass course of 150° as we left Stuart island for Roche Harbor, but the current is so strong he's had to correct to 90°. He says even so we may not make it into the pass between Henry Island and northern San Juan. The water roils and ripples. We see it and hear it.

We succeed. The water approach to Roche Harbor is picturesque. You see the shining, tall white form of the little chapel (supposedly the only privately owned Catholic Church in the west) and the round green horse chestnut trees. There's also the major, bulky white of the restaurant and of the hotel; the wide-spaced white of ten workmen's cottages; the brown accent of a log skid and a "boom" where logs float, ready for market; and the gray masonry of the lime kilns, which would be a puzzle if you didn't already know the story here.

British soldiers apparently were the first to successfully produce lime in the San Juan Islands, though earlier there'd been a doomed operation at the Lime Kiln Lighthouse area, now Sam Buck's Carefree subdivision. August Hibbard, the operator there, was stabbed to death; so was his successor. Whiskey smuggling seems to have accompanied the quarrying of that particular limestone. Large-scale lime production waited till 1886 and the arrival of John Stafford McMillin: midwestern, a lawyer, and a steadfast Republican associated with the Tacoma Lime Works. He was drawn to Roche Harbor by a limestone ledge fronted with deep water ideal for shipping.

Thirteen kilns in a double row were turning out lime by 1890. It was the biggest operation west of the Mississippi, replete with its own ships and orders from as far away as Alaska, Hawaii, and Panama. Nearly 250 people lived at Roche Harbor, a 4,000-acre, one-industry town with company housing, company store, company church, company saloon, and company cemetery. This wasn't some dreadful tyranny. It's simply a system from the past that now has poured through the hourglass of time. McMillin died in 1936. Production dropped and finally the "inexhaustible" lime deposit played out. Reuben Tarte, a Seattle boating enthusiast, bought the facilities and turned them into a model resort accessible by ferry and then road, by water in your own boat, or by small plane.

The ruins of a dozen lime operations remain on Orcas Island, seven here on San Juan, two on Henry Island, one on Crane Island. The masonry construction of a developing West couldn't go forward without lime. The operation at Roche Harbor even provided cash for settlers throughout the islands: men cut wood and brought it here to fire the kilns. That scalping of the forest created massive problems. Look at historic photographs of the British encampment and you see deep-draft sailing ships tied to a dock leading out from the

blockhouse and formal garden. Try sailing in there now and your fathometer warns you to give up. The middle of the bay is barely more than six feet deep and it shoals rapidly toward shore. It has silted in. Time equals change.

Yesterday I talked with Charlie Nash, the Friday Harbor postmaster beloved for his impish smile and friendly words for all—a quiet, modest, true gentleman whose San Juan roots go back five generations. One side of the family came from Maine, where they were shipbuilders; the other side arrived from Virginia after the Civil War.

"Most of my schoolmates have left the islands," Charlie says. "There wasn't any work except in the pea cannery. Now some are coming back as retirees. Tourism really goes pretty far back. I was raised in the retail drug business, and it depended on tourists. Water transport was good here; no highway or planes, but we had steamers. They'd come right in and you rolled your cargo aboard. Agriculture was big, and timber found a good cash market too, mostly in San Francisco.

"The movement-out from the islands started before World War II. The movement-in is still pretty new."

Charlie never left. He liked the water and started fishing, working in winter for cash as a bookkeeper or credit manager. His gillnetter is well named *Betcha*. Anything that affects the islands interests him, which accounts for his renown as the eagle expert of the county. In 1960 people started worrying about bald eagles and DDT and the National Audubon society asked for volunteers to look into the matter. Charlie made a January count. A couple years later a Hungarian refugee enrolled at the University of British Columbia arrived to see if the islands would be a good place for a doctoral dissertation on bald eagles. Charlie realized he couldn't tell the man where the nests were, so from a chartered plane he scouted for them and located four or five nests with chicks that one day.

Around the same time an article came out claiming there were at most only five eagle nests left in the whole state of Washington. Since Charlie knew of more than that in the San Juans alone, he started to keep a regular census from the air. "I wanted to take fifteen to twenty nests and watch them through the year," he says. "Do the birds stay around? Migrate? Fall out of the nest?"

Some eagles are hypersensitive to human intrusion and may abandon a nest if people come within 600 feet of it. Others don't much care. All are protected by federal law—rather to the annoyance of some San Juan people. There are at least forty active nests in the county and occasionally construction work has been halted by the arrival of eagles (which for the most part leave the islands in summer, start returning in late October). No human disturbance is permissable within a quarter mile of a nest, and since bald eagles — as do people — prefer to live with a clear view of the sea, there is some irritation. There's even an instance of someone cutting down a nest tree within a newly platted tract, a federal offense under the Endangered Species Act.

Charlie Nash knows the eagles by territory and personality. There's the pair he calls The Lovers because they sit perched side by side on the nest. And there are the ones he had to rescue from the water. They'd locked talons in a courtship flight and couldn't disentangle.

European rabbits, long ago turned loose on San Juan, today provide a food base for hawks, owls, and golden eagles. But people need to beware of twisting an ankle in their burrows, particularly in the Cattle Point area.

Farming came to San Juan in 1853 with the British owned Hudson's Bay Company.
Products today range from beef and wool to poultry and eggs, fruit and berries.

Seeing them in the water, landowners phoned Charlie. He borrowed a boat and lifted the pair from the water.

Why bother? Alaska and British Columbia have large eagle populations, perhaps 50,000 individual eagles in Alaska alone. But for the forty-eight states as a whole, there are only 1,000 pairs of breeding eagles. There's an aura about the birds. They focus questions of "endangered-ness," of living in balance with the earth.

Similar concern centers on killer whales, which really should be called by their species name "orca" to get away from an inaccurate connotation of ferocity. We don't speak of killer cats, though pet tabbies are notorious for stalking birds; nor do we think of killer kingfishers or killer spiders — or killer man. I talked about orcas with Peter Capen, executive director of the Friday Harbor Whale Museum. Northwest Coast Indians revered the whales as much as the eagle—maybe even more among local Indians. But we modern humans, creatures of the land, have lost acquaintance with the swimmers even more than with the fliers. Scientists now are restoring touch.

By photographing every orca seen in the inland waterway from Washington's Neah Bay and Olympia to British Columbia's cannery town of Namu, researchers learned to identify individual whales according to differences in the white "saddle" patch behind the dorsal fin and notches in the fin itself. That done, they began noticing that certain individuals characteristically appeared together in family groups called pods. Three such pods totalling about eighty whales belong to Puget Sound and the straits of Georgia and Juan de Fuca. Farther north there are twelve pods with more than 130 individuals. The two communities don't mix, though southern pods frequently visit each other and northern pods do the same. Additionally, there are fifteen pods with about forty-seven whales that stay on the move and don't seem to ever mix with any of the resident pods. Why? Nobody knows.

Quite astonishingly, each pod has its own repertoire of about thirty-two clicks and whistles and metallic-sounding shrieks. Furthermore, the dialect used by southern pods differs from that of northern pods. What they're saying isn't known; maybe it's a constant affirmation of togetherness.

Regardless, the distinct calls are so clear that experts can recognize individual pods underwater by the sound coming through a hydrophone. When two pods are swimming together, each holds to its own preferred set of calls, though it knows all the calls within its dialect. Even when a whale is captured and taught tricks, it doesn't change its repertoire. Recordings from Marineland, California, show that the two British Columbia whales there haven't changed their calls. Their vocalizations still match those of pod-mates in the wild, who may well be kin. Are the captives whistling and shrieking descriptions of what it feels like to snatch fish from a man's mouth and chase a ball? Or is it nostalgia for the good old days of chasing tomcod and squid? Whatever, nobody really understands. Catching and transporting a single orca costs more than $100,000, but tickets at the gate readily turn that outlay into profit. This our species does understand.

The Whale Museum, upstairs in the Odd Fellows Hall in Friday Harbor (second oldest building in town), opened in 1979, "the product of 400 volunteers and $200 in cash," as Peter Capen puts it. A large, strong man still young, Peter is an idealist wrapped in a pragmatist's clothing. "The aquariums that capture orcas say they study them scientifically, as well as teach them tricks," he says. "But what kind of life is it for one or two socially active whales confined in a tank? We believe that every study aquarium officials claim could also be done in the wild.

"These waters are one of the two places in the world where orca research can be done in the field — and there's no question we see things no aquarium behaviorist will ever see. The way orcas sleep in close body contact, for example. Or how when two pods meet, they first swim through one another like some drill routine of a high school marching band. It's in the wild that we see extra females escorting mothers with new calves, acting for all the world like loving aunties or like apprentices learning about infant care. It's here that we see the whales play in *their* way, not some human trick. They splash each other, and trail kelp fronds held in their mouths or draped against their fins.

"Of course certain things can be learned at a zoo — the controlled environment and all that. But such an approach seems to us a bit lazy compared with meeting the orcas in their own realm and studying what is normal without intruding on them." These are animals up to twenty-five feet long, weighing five to seven tons. They're found mostly in temperate oceans but range from pole to pole and even swim up rivers such as the Loire, Rhine, Thames — and the Columbia. One was harpooned 110 miles in from the mouth of the Columbia River a few years ago. It evidently had been living on carp. "The Indians knew about orcas. So should we. And the San Juans are an ideal place for studying them."

The words echo a statement made by David Duggins the evening we stopped at Yellow Island: "The San Juans are the perfect place for a biology station like Friday Harbor Laboratories. You're out in the field — surrounded by your work — yet you have sophisticated equipment and colleagues from all over the world." This summer alone a biologist from Portsmouth, England, is studying the ontogeny of the ascospore appendange in marine *Pyrenomycetes*—the life history of a certain seaweed — and nobody is asking whether a pharmaceutical house cares about what he discovers. His turn at the scanning electron microscope and the battery of laboratory computers is assured regardless. A scientist from the People's Republic of China wants to study marine larvae, and the lab head doesn't mention that Western scientists have studied and written up such material for decades. Maybe a mind with a different cultural background will see something everybody else has overlooked.

The laboratories, administered as part of the University of Washington, began in 1904 as the Puget Sound Marine Station. They, too, had a post office problem: letters would end up at the Port Townsend military station, the marine labs confused with the U.S. Marine Corps. In 1913 the name changed to Puget Sound Biological Station, and, ironically, the labs settled the following year onto a surplus military reservation turned over by the federal government: the present idyllic campus. There are historic pictures of women students in high-necked blouses and long skirts dipping nets into tidepools; and early-day student journals reporting, for example, "Professor Kincaid warned all that work would begin at 4:00 the next morning and the bell would ring then. Everyone looked at their neighbor to see if he was serious." He was.

Students still come to Friday Harbor Labs, but research, more than teaching, is the prime function (and the ideal climate for graduate students). The mission is akin to a biological think tank. Pure research. The kind of work done to advance knowledge regardless of what — or when — useful applications may evolve. This biology station continues the work of disciplined intellects, who are allowed to free-wheel in pursuit of answers and thereby turn up new questions. From Galileo to Darwin to Einstein such minds have been asking, "Why?" Everybody wins in this approach, except perhaps the scientist wearily performing an experiment for the thousandth time.

Dr. Dennis Willows, who heads the labs, comments: "Let's assume you're not sympathetic to the idea that knowledge is good for its own sake. You want a different answer — an applied answer. It's there. Every worthwhile development in biomedicine and every technological advance is based on years of basic research at a place like this. If society is to be healthy, if we're to compete in the industrial world, then we'd better be doing this research for all we're worth. There's no choice but to invest in understanding the biological and physical phenomena around us. Others are doing it. If we don't, we're well and truly lost."

Dr. Willows is a lean man with an intense, harried look. You sense the urgency he feels just by seeing him at his desk. I once read an article of his dealing with a certain foot-long sea slug, or nudibranch, called *Tritonia diomedia*. It has brain cells so large some can be seen with the unaided eye, others resolved with a simple, low-power microscope. Moreover, cell colors vary from oranges and yellows to various whites differing in relative brightness. In other words, you can watch on a cell-by-cell basis as the brain receives input from the nervous system and organizes and transmits a response. Dr. Willows determined which body cells receive the message of a sun starfish's touch — the principal predator of the nudibranch — and then he traced the paths within the nervous system used for sending that worrisome news to the brain. "I repeated the test for each cell several times in different animals," he writes. "The exploration entailed a large number of trials — more than 20,000 of them, in fact."

That was just the beginning. Next step was to reverse the experiment, following from individual brain cells back to muscle cells. After that, Dr. Willows checked within the brain itself to see whether cells there communicated with each other, passing the message along, or whether each had to get its own message directly. Who besides Dennis Willows really cares? It may be any of us, or our descendants, if someday a learning-disabled child finds the hookups for reading, or a stroke-paralyzed oldster learns to walk again.

For several reasons the infinite lifeforms of the sea are ideal for uncovering basic biological truths. Many are organized along rather simple lines, which helps a researcher sort through more quickly to cause-effect relationships. Furthermore, huge nerve and muscle cells are common among many marine species, the largest within the entire animal kingdom. Fundamental pieces belonging to the jigsaw puzzle of life eventually become clear by studying how these cells convulse or relax in response to drugs or electrical signals. Scien-

tists can trace errors in the DNA "blueprints" of a deformed sand dollar or segmented worm, and study how a starfish reforms an arm of its own but rejects transplanted tissue. They can tag the invertebrates and seaweeds in a tidepool for identification, then study the competition for space, or add a pollutant and note which organisms survive, which succumb. Answers to the puzzle of why cells and nervous systems react as they do carries over from species to species. Knowledge advances. Human medicine improves. The diversity of the San Juans diffuses into the wellbeing of us all.

Nudibranchs. Whales. Eagles. In the San Juans you sense the time that stretches from when glacier ice was scratching and polishing the bedrock of the islands and veneering them with gravel to John McMillin's recognition of the lime potential at Roche Harbor; from Indians' reef netting to the County Comprehensive Plan.

The San Juan islands are where you watch from a ferry while a Franciscan nun operates the gangplank, and where your fiberglass craft travels alongside a wooden local boat heading for Waldron with lumber and chickens and stovepipe. You can bike, hike, clam, fish, sail, row. Sleep in a tent or a motel or a mansion. Watch birds or sip a sunset brandy while the Roche Harbor resort staff lowers the American, Canadian, and British flags and loudspeakers play *The Star-Spangled Banner, Oh, Canada,* and *God Save the Queen.*

The sun sizzles into the water west of our anchorage. Flags are folded; the young staff members march off. Whoops and boat whistle toots sound all around. Then there's silence. We see stars, where man probes with the same curiosity as that at work on a different scale within individual living cells. Slowly Louis rows our dinghy. A seal surfaces, its round head a discernible form gliding parallel to us, totally silent. With each pull of the oars, minute organisms light their bioluminescent lamps, and we progress across a sea surface seemingly as much light as liquid.

No wonder Robert Moran — industrialist, twice-elected Seattle mayor — came to Rosario to die and instead found life. No wonder our ninety-year-old friend Herb Evison recognizes landmarks unseen for sixty years, which he's never before viewed from the air. These islands etch themselves onto the mind and nurture the soul.

The first criterion of San Juan-ness is that there be no bridge. You must come by water or air. Once arrived, it's okay to walk or bike or drive—as well as to sail, paddle, row, and motor.

Above: Once the waters swarmed with smugglers carrying illicit cargo from opium to Canadian wool; the coves where they hid now play host to pleasure craft—and tranquility. *Overleaf:* Large ships to and from Vancouver sail through Haro Strait, the international boundary.

Above: On San Juan Island, gardens add grace to Hotel de Haro, where luminaries, such as Presidents Theodore Roosevelt and William Howard Taft, once stayed. *Right:* Friday Harbor is both county seat for the islands and a busy port. *Overleaf:* Near Friday Harbor, coves and rocks bright with lichen invite exploring.

Bucolic farm fields and fishboats tied at the dock or plying their trade contribute to the charm beloved by island residents and visitors.

Above: A member of the mustard family grown for its oily seed spreads its lemon-yellow blossoms across a farmer's field. *Left:* Friday Harbor serves as base for gillnetters (foreground), purse seiners, and trollers—the present-day successors of Indian canoe reef-netters. Some boats venture far beyond the relatively calm island waters.

Above: Ferries give year-round connections between the islands and mainland Washington, as well as Vancouver Island, British Columbia. *Right:* Gray days are few in summer owing to the "rain shadow" of the Olympic Mountains, which blocks Pacific Ocean storm clouds from reaching the islands.

Drawing official lines on San Juan charts very nearly set off war in 1859. All might have been well except that nobody specified which channel marked the international boundary, Rosario or Haro.

Above: On rare snowy days winter turns sea and sky to steely blue-gray, and mariners who have ventured out welcome the wink of Lime Kiln Lighthouse. *Left:* The small blockhouse at Garrison Bay remains from the nineteenth-century British and American tensions, origin of the rallying cry of "Fifty-four Forty or Fight."

Above: The local postmaster knows island bald eagles by personality. He calls one pair The Lovers because they sit side by side; another pair, he rescued from the water after they locked talons in courtship flight and couldn't disentangle. *Right:* At American Camp the two surviving buildings are quarters for officers (shown here) and for a laundress. Nearby, the earthern redoubt remains evident.

Timelessness is the soothing essence of these islands, a siren call luring admirers both resident and transient. The question is how well the loveliness can keep pace with the lovers.

Above: Small islands closely clustered mean limitless coves for anchoring, permissable even offshore from private land. *Left:* Summer days offer shirtsleeve passage through labyrinthine waterways. *Overleaf:* Marinas, such as this large one at Friday Harbor, provide rental boats and docks.

Above: The allure of the shore is to walk, wade, dig clams, beachcomb, peer into tidepools, and otherwise stretch the soul. *Right:* Climb to the top of Young Hill on San Juan for a view of outlying islands which lead like stepping stones to Canadian waters. *Overleaf:* Deer Harbor is one of three major inlets notching the coast of Orcas Island.

Above: Blacktop leads to the 2,409-foot summit of Mount Constitution, a steep, six-mile drive replete with hairpin curves and switchbacks. Reward? A 360-degree panorama, including this view across the Strait of Georgia to Mount Baker. *Left:* The distant Olympics backdrop Lopez Island, as seen from Mount Constitution.

Buck deer still in velvet browse the edge of a farmer's field—no problem in this instance but a decided nuisance where fruit crops or household gardens are ripening. Deer easily swim from island to island.

The islands are a richly varied realm full of broad scenes and intimate details, all interwoven into a human tapestry.

Agriculture once was the economic base of the San Juan Islands. Pasturage, hay, and grain continue a major role allowing pastoral charm to remain high among the islands' primary values.

Mount Baker looms virginal in the distance, an icy wedge catching the pink of sunset and contrasting it with the blue of islands and waters.

Above: Geologists haven't finished piecing together the puzzle of the islands' formation. Parts have migrated here as ocean plates shifted position, a phenomenon that also results in volcanoes. *Right:* Orcas Island's East Sound was sculpted by glacier ice 15,000 years ago during the Pleistocene Epoch.

Above: Eastsound village has served as Orcas' hub since the 1880s. Many original buildings remain, some now catering to tourists, others to residents. *Left:* The tiny community of Olga, on Orcas Island's southern tip, can be reached by water or road. Bicyclists especially savor rest and refreshment here.

Above: The view from the porch of Rosario, the Moran mansion, is now accessible to all. *Right:* Appropriate for a successful shipbuilder, Robert Moran salvaged the figure-head of the clippership *America*. Built in Massachusetts, it wrecked here in 1914. *Overleaf:* The mansion's organ has 1,972 pipes. No musician himself, Moran operated it like a player piano and accepted the praise of unsuspecting guests.

Above: Robert Moran donated land for a state park. Its forested uplands are dotted by lakes and laced with streams and waterfalls, such as Cascade Falls. *Left:* Rosario is listed on the National Register of Historic Places, assuring protection of the mansion's facade. Rooms now are rented to resort guests. *Overleaf:* Moran State Park embraces the mountainous heartland of Orcas Island.

Above: East Sound (foreground) nearly splits apart the land masses of east and west Orcas Island. *Right:* A fifty-foot observation tower atop Mount Constitution dates from the 1930s. Crews quarried blocks of Orcas Island sandstone and built—completely illogically—a supposed facsimile of an eleventh-century Russian fortification.

Above: Fleece from Lopez Island sheep ends up as handspun yarn and knitwear; residents on other islands specialize in weaving. *Left:* Madrones indicate bedrock lying close beneath the surface. Bark is naturally scaly. Leaves stay green all year.

The Richardson settlement boasted the first post office on Lopez and the first meeting hall—though claiming the hall as first disregards the plank houses of the Indians, 400 feet long by 40 feet wide.

Above: The Richardson Store at the southern end of Lopez Island is the place to indulge yourself in a huge, justly famous ice cream cone. *Right:* Eons of tumbling in the surf make the stones of Agate Beach look like misshapen Easter eggs. A park provides beach access and picnic tables.

Walk the road leading to Lopez Village and sit on the porch of Holly B's Bakery with a chocolate croissant and fresh coffee, and you rejoice in some of the changes imported into the San Juan Islands.

Above: Fog lifts off the water beyond an abandoned farmstead at Lopez Village. Shakes loosening from the roof peak may herald an end for the aging house. *Left:* On the outskirts of Lopez Village an old red schoolhouse is now the community library; other one-room schools in the islands still serve their original purpose.

These islands etch themselves onto the mind and nurture the soul. Their myriad lifeforms and patterns give peace.

Above: Purple shore crabs scuttle off, apparently able to see an intruder's approach. Pigments shift within the retina, adapting the crab's eyes to day or night vision. Diatoms and algae scraped from rocks provide food. *Right:* Bedrock outcrops and tiny offshore islets characterize southern Lopez. *Overleaf:* Summer paints the pink and green of wild beach pea onto the blue tranquility of Lopez Island's Fisherman Bay.

Above: Ray Spencer built this cabin around the time of the First World War. In 1978 State Parks officials had it rebuilt as a public shelter. *Left:* Scuba divers are rewarded with high visibility in cold waters and an abundant marine life including abalone, lingcod, and colorful invertebrates. *Overleaf:* Spencer Spit builds steadily outward. In time it will join tiny Frost Island (background) to eastern Lopez Island.

Above: A venerable reef-net boat, typical of a special San Juans method of fishing, sits in front of Shaw Island's combined historical museum and library. *Right:* Shaw residents donated land at Indian Cove for a county park, a generous act laced with a hope of stopping trespass on private land.

Above: Modern houses with wide decks and glassy walls crown low points that offer both wide vistas and easy access to the water. *Left:* Cabins of logs augmented by lumber testify to pioneering days which here started nebulously in the 1850s, climaxed from the 1880s to early 1900s.

With careful ritual and great ingenuity, Salish Indians living along these waterways intercepted the salmon and welcomed them, calling them Elder Brother and Honored Ones.

Above: Modern reef-netters operate where shallow passages concentrate salmon runs.
Right: Every beach holds flotsam (wreckage) and jetsam (material thrown overboard), from hatch covers to curious bottles and useful pieces of wood. Walking the shore to see what the tides have left is a deep seated tradition among all islanders.

Above: Let a breeze stir and sailors' hearts rejoice, especially while aboard a vessel as graceful as this cruising ketch. *Left:* When salmon pass through San Juan Islands' waters en route to spawn up the Fraser River, fishermen head out to test mind, radar, depth finder, and—in this case—gillnet against the instincts of the fish.

Lummi Island bounds eastern Hale Passage. The Spanish explorer Eliza called the island Pacheco, part of the name of the viceroy of Mexico. The American Navy lieutenant Charles Wilkes named it McLoughlin, for the Hudson's Bay Company factor. The present name is for the Lummi Indians, whose island it was.

Above: Lummi beaches offer solitude and a chance to gear your mind to nature's pace.
Overleaf: Captain George Vancouver, sailing the San Juans in 1792, wrote: "Nothing can be more striking than the beauty of these waters... without any danger whatever for the length of this internal navigation."

Above: Drift logs form a sculpture garden on Lummi Island beaches. *Right:* Starfish have no head, unusual for such large animals. The mouth is on the underside of the central disk; "arms" are lined with tiny tube feet. *Overleaf:* Sea anemones' green color comes from algae living in their tissue. The algae photosynthesize food useful to the anemone; the anemone's waste fertilizes the algae.

Each pod of whales has its own dialect wholly distinct from that of any other group. Even in captivity they continue their particular vocalizations.

Above: "These waters are…a place where orca research can be done in the field," says the director of the San Juan whale museum. "And there's no question we see things no aquarium behaviorist will ever see." *Left:* The sandstone of Waldron Island's Point Disney was quarried during the early 1900s for uses as diverse as the Columbia River jetty and Seattle's stone streets.

The future? All who live in the San Juans or visit them notice the change of the last decade—a doubling of the population—and all wonder what lies ahead.

Above: The Waldron mail boat links the island with the world beyond the San Juans.
Right: Prevost Harbor on Stuart Island is lined by stone that formed as layers of sediment hardened and, over time, tilted and folded into rhythmic ribbons.

Above: "Overall, the pace of human life has so quickened that one generation has few templates to pass to the next. So people seek a simpler life by moving to the San Juans, or at least coming to visit," comments an afficionado. *Left:* The land surface of the San Juan Islands totals less than 200 square miles scattered across an area twenty-five miles wide which constitutes San Juan County.

On Matia Island there lived a hermit who would row two-and-a-half miles to Orcas, then walk another two miles to Eastsound to buy groceries and to socialize. He had no dock, so when the captain of the weekly mail boat had letters, he tooted as he neared Matia, and the hermit rowed out to get his mail and gossip.

Twin outboard motors lift power boats to planing speed, shortening the distances old-timers traveled by muscle-power and squeezing island adventure into available weekend and vacation time.

The shells of cockles, as of other clams, typically show ring on ring of growth, products of each feeding. The process is much like the more familiar one by which trees grow yearly rings of new wood.

Above: Pelagic cormorants nest in rock crevices on many isolated San Juan islands, typically surrounded by other nearby nesters such as glaucous winged gulls. *Overleaf:* A cove at Matia State Park provides easy beach access.

The San Juans are hard to define. It depends on whether you're thinking of high tide or low. There are 457 islands, rocks, and reefs at high tide and 768 at low.

Above: All of Decatur Island, as of many small islands within the San Juans, is privately owned. Two coves, however, provide excellent public anchorage. *Right:* Waterworn sandstone at Fox Cove on Sucia Island includes an impressive eight-foot "mushroom." The area is a marine state park reached only by water. *Overleaf:* Honeycombed stone lines the entrance to Patos Island's main bay.

The span of boats in the San Juans began with Indians' cedar dugout canoes and evolved to modern vessels with powerful engines and radars that see through fog and night.

Above: "Today people are trying to find themselves—or lose themselves—I'm not sure which," says a longtime island resident. "This place attracts 'em all." *Left:* Patos Island features an abandoned lighthouse, a small park, no roads or landing strip, and ample room for easing the psyche.

PATOS ISLAND

SUCIA ISLAND

STUART ISLAND

EAST SOUND

HENRY ISLAND

WALDRON ISLAND

SPIEDEN ISLAND

FRIDAY HARBOR

SHAW ISLAND

LOPEZ VILLAGE

SAN JUAN ISLAND

SAN JUAN ISLANDS